POEMS OF A MUSICAL FLAVOUR

POEMS OF A MUSICAL FLAVOUR

VOLUME 1

TIARA KING

♫ Royal Star Publishing ♫

Notes on Life is an imprint of Royal Star Publishing
www.royalstarpublishing.com.au

First edition paperback published in 2018
All Rights Reserved, Copyright ©Tiara King 2018

Trade Paperback ISBN: 978-1-925683-73-8
Case Laminate Hardcover ISBN: 978-1-922307-18-7
E-book ISBN: 978-1-925683-03-5
A catalogue record for this book is available from the National Library of Australia.

Cover design: Royal Star Publishing and Odyssey Books
Cover photos: Girl: EzepovDmitry/Shutterstock.com
Background: JBOY/Shutterstock.com
Typesetting in Minion Pro by Royal Star Publishing

The right of Tiara King to be identified as the author of her work has been asserted.
This book is a work of fiction. Any references to real people or real locales are used fictitiously, and any resemblance to actual events, locales or persons, living or dead, is entirely coincidental.
No part of this publication may be reproduced, published, performed in public or communicated to the public in any form or by any means without prior written permission of Royal Star Publishing.
Requests to publish work from this book should be sent to:
authors@royalstarpublishing.com.au

CONTENTS

Introduction	1
1989	**7**
Be True To Me – Ballad	8
Leave Me Alone	10
In The Heat Of The Night – Ballad	12
Crimes Of Passion	14
Rock Music	16
Movin' Along – Ballad	18
The Heavens Are Burning	20
Danger Zone	22
Beware	24
Wanted	26
Here Today, Gone Tomorrow	28
You're On Your Way – Ballad	30
On Top	32
Playing Up	34
It's Our Home	36
Echo Of Your Love – Ballad	38
Who's Sorry Now?	40
Let's Party	42
1990	**45**
Only In My Dreams	46
Busy Signal	48
Truly Outrageous	50
Competing To Win	52

Win Or Lose – Rap	54
Forever In Time – Ballad	56
Before Day Breaks	58
Eyes Of Fire	60
Destiny	62
Crazy Heart – Ballad	64
Flame In My Heart	66
In Love With You	68
Follow Your Dreams	70
Lovin' Fool	72
Love In Your Eyes	74
As Time Goes By	76
Shelter In The Storm – Ballad	78
Don't Shed A Tear	80
Wish Upon A Star – Ballad	82
Let's Rock This Town	84
Once In A Lifetime	86
Now And Forever – Ballad	88
Lovin' You	90
Just Too Late – Ballad	92
Searching	94
Burning Up	96
Tell Me Now	98
Get It Together	100
Treat Me Right	102
Together Again	104
Games Of Love	106
Broken Dreams – Ballad	108
Come Back	110
Imagine	112
Life In The Fast Lane	114

Countin' The Days	116
Temptations	118
A Cry In The Night	120
You'd Better Stop	122
Devil In Disguise	124
Red Hot Love	126
Something To Dream – Ballad	128
Love Is An Emotion	130
Walls Of Fire	132
Opposite Extremes	134
An Angel's Dreams – Ballad	136
Without You – Ballad	138
Forgotten Dreams – Ballad	140
Messenger Of Hope – Ballad	142
Race Against Time	144
Every Time We Say Goodbye	146
I Need Someone	148
About the Author	150
Other Titles	152

INTRODUCTION

My writing career can be traced back to primary school, year 7 to be exact, when I wrote and published my first book. After that I wrote and published a second and third for school and then for some reason, fancied myself as a song writer. I wrote lyrics, more on that in a moment, and wrote "songs" because I wanted to be a singer. But after seven years I stopped and that was replaced ten years later by longer "songs" called novels. That's when books and short stories came. Then came the idea to write out and print up these lyrics of mine into books…

It took me three weeks to write out 639 sets of song lyrics and I was definite that I had 700… maybe I need to add to that 639… I even wrote songs about child abuse, heavy lyrics by my standard back in 1994 when I was 20, and probably still very relevant today. There are also a few things I realise now, at the ripe old age of 44 (at the time of this printing), that I would not have realised back then.

1 - Most of the songs had the same lyrics, so I seemed to plagiarise myself a lot.

2 - The lyrics were incredibly young-sounding at the beginning.

3 - I wrote the way so many teens did back then.

4 - I was way ahead of my years and the time because of the topics I wrote about, and surprisingly, they are still very and incredibly relevant, if not more dominant, now.

My lyrics were young because I started writing them when I was 15 in 1989. It was year ten in high school, I played the drums and piano, wore a funky blue knitted jumper with a stave on it with the first line of Funky Town and thought I was hot. I also wanted to be a singer...

I wanted to be Australia's version of Debbie Gibson and I'm listening to her first album, *Out of the Blue*, as I write this (I love '80s music more than anything). I loved everything about her. Her funky clothes to the Swatch watches she wore. And when she moved into her new mansion, I wanted *it* and everything else. That's why she inspired me with her lyrics and melodies. She did it all. It also didn't hurt that the only time she ever toured Australia was with my favourite Aussie band, Indecent Obsession. I also wrote many a song about them. She even had a thing with the lead singer. Oooooohhhhhh.

Debbie Gibson was huge, along with Tiffany, Kylie and Dannii Minogue, Indecent Obsession, Yazz, Kim Wilde, and an abundance of others in 1989. There was '80s bubble-gum/pop blasting from every radio and TV. Even Jem and the Holograms got a go (gotta love the '80s). Debbie was the inspiration for my lyrics, so the early ones are very similar in a young teenage style of the '80s. They aged as I did, but I stopped writing after 7 years as I'd moved on, but did write one song in 2002. But Debbie is very much in there, in inspiration for song titles, or lines or phrases, as are so many other artists who gave me the idea for a funky tune or romantic ballad.

When going back over the decades of music, lyrics were incredibly simple, be it '50s, '60s, '70s or '80s. Come the '90s it changed. Grunge came in and lyrics became down right weird, and you'd read them and go 'what were they on when they wrote this?' These days it's different again. Between Kelly Clarkson, P!nk, Lady Gaga, Taylor Swift, and so many other females and males, not to mention bands, lyrics have become harder, edgier, and downright far too sexy for the teens singing them. I occasionally wonder how they come up with such adult stuff.

Back in the day, lyrics were young and innocent, now, they're far too sexual. I definitely don't know if I could write any now, the lyrics would be older, more mature, but writing books gives me a longer platform to get the story across. Not sure I could do it in four verses, a chorus, and a bridge anymore. But you never know. Writing them all up gave me inspiration… And you know I can't *not* write something… With everything else I already write and the books yet to be written...*something* is going to come out at some stage.

I wrote from 1989 to 2002 then that was it. Four years later I wrote my first novel, and I think my lyrics made way for that. I even wrote song trilogies which have stood me in good stead for writing the book trilogy I wrote in 2016. Lyrics were clearly my training for bigger and longer stories, which songs are. They are stories of love, pain, hurt, heartache etc. Just listen to country songs. The dog dies, the wife leaves and the ute breaks down. Songs are full of it and many times lyrics are simple.

Remember all those really poppy songs from the '80s? Try Stock, Aitken and Waterman songs, Kylie Minogue, Jason Donovan, Bananarama, Sonia, any UK '80s pop act had one of their songs and they were all done to formula. Two verses, chorus, two verses, chorus, bridge, chorus to end. The music was what sucked you in, it was up tempo, poppy and danceable. But analyse the lyrics and they were the most teenager-ish ridiculous things around. Yet they meant so much at the time when we were young, but reading back over them as adults they are just silly and childish. Remember B*Witched's *Rollercoaster* and Kylie's *I Should Be So Lucky*? Enough said!

But that's what makes a pop song, and that's what I wrote. Young pop lyrics from a 15-22 year old that didn't know any better and wasn't experienced at anything we call life. Like now.

Did my lyrics get older and more mature? Sort

of. You can see the progression into '94-'96. Around this time Alanis Morissette came out and I desperately wished I could write a song like her. I didn't have her angst, but I tried. I'm not sure I succeeded. There are a few good sets of lyrics in the last years and some of my song titles were freakin' awesome, like *Brunettes Look Best in Red*, *Ginger Elle*, *Cool Fred* and *Firenze*. A line from someone else's song, or an Impulse body spray name (big body spray label over here that's been around forever) was all for the taking.

I did songs about politics, the world, generation x (the Spice Girls ripped me off a few years later with that one, lol). No topic was not written about... that I remember.

But for me, life took a turn and here we are, nearly 30 years later, and I still don't sing or write song lyrics. Instead, I write books and short stories under three names and maybe these songs, these lyrics, were the beginning of my ability to come up with unusual titles and strange stories (although I'm sure all of my English teachers at school could attest to the fact I did that even earlier), and writing a trilogy of songs as I do a trilogy of books.

Thank you to all the muses, guides, helpers, inspirational musicians and singers that gave me the lines, the titles, the ideas for these songs. I honour you and dedicate these books to all of you.

This book, and the five following, is a culmination of my love of music.

I've written a line or two about the artist or song

that inspired me with the lyrics and why, on many of the songs, most of which are pop songs unless otherwise stated, and let's hope I won't get sued for using someone as inspiration (so many lawsuits going on these days). But jokes aside, I was young and a teenager and these songs are what I came up with. And now I'm publishing them just for the fun of it, and to have more books under my name on my author page, *and* on my bookshelf.

Whether or not you enjoy them is up to you, but remember, if you plagiarise me, you're being sued... and no, I'm not joking...

1989

Let's start with the song lyrics I wrote in 1989. I was 15 years old, living in Adelaide, South Australia, and I wrote 18 songs. I started writing late in the year, I was playing the drums in my music class end of year musical, so not only had I developed a love of music through the year, I was also majorly crushing on Debbie Gibson and wanted to *be* her.

BE TRUE TO ME
ballad

This song was originally called Fairy Tales. I can't remember why I changed it and rewrote it all those years ago, but I did. Maybe to make it lyrically better, but then to me, it must have been bad for one of my first. I have a feeling it may have been influenced by an Indecent Obsession song, *Never Really Loved You*, but I didn't write it down anywhere so can only go by the vague familiarity of the lyrics.

V1
You told me that you loved me,
But that seemed like so long ago,
You locked all your love away,
And I still wait for it to show.

V2
You keep telling me lies,
And I keep believing you,
Though I should know better,
I always stick by you.

CHORUS
Why can't you Be True To Me?
I love you so why can't you see?
Please Be True To Me,
You hold the key, Oh, boy can't you see…

Please Be True To Me.

V3
I never get to see you no more,
But you say you want me,
How come we're never together?
You say you wanna be with me.

V4
You keep telling me lies,
And I keep believing you,
Though I don't have to listen,
I'll always be there for you.

CHORUS

BRIDGE
You had told me you loved me,
You had told me you cared,
Though I should've known better,
I still really cared.

LEAVE ME ALONE

This song was inspired by Indecent Obsession's *Why Do People Fall in Love*, which was a B-side to one of their first singles. I rewrote this song too, again, don't remember why, but I did.

V1
I've had enough of trying,
When all you do is walk away,
People never listen to me,
I just wanna be left for a day.

V2
I just can't do nothing right,
You wanna stay for the night,
I keep telling you to just…
Leave Me Alone.

CHORUS
Leave Me Alone,
I don't wanna talk to you,
Leave Me Alone,
I don't wanna be with you,
Leave Me Alone,
I don't wanna see you,
Leave Me Alone,
Why don't you Leave Me Alone.

V3
I think I'm going crazy,
I just wanna be on my own,
I want to get you out of my life,
I just wanna be left alone.

V4
You keep hanging round,
I never want to see you,
Why can't you Leave Me Alone,
I don't want to be with you.

CHORUS

REPEAT V2
I just can't do nothing right,
You wanna stay for the night,
I keep telling you to just…
Leave Me Alone.

IN THE HEAT OF THE NIGHT
ballad

V1
As our bodies moves closer,
This is all like a dream,
As our love grows stronger,
It means a lot to me.

V2
I'll always wanna be with you,
You know my love is true,
I want us to be together,
Even if it means forever.

CHORUS
In The Heat of the Night,
I wanna spend my life with you,
In The Heat of the Night,
I wanna keep on seeing you,
I wanna be with you,
I'll always love you true,
In The Heat of the Night.

V3
As our night together ends,
You tell me you love me,
As our time together ends,
I ask you why can't you see.

V4
I love you so much,
And I wanna be with you,
You say it can't last forever,
But I know that ain't true.

CHORUS

REPEAT V2
I'll always wanna be with you,
You know my love is true,
I want us to be together,
Even if it means forever.

CRIMES OF PASSION

V1
On the day I saw you,
You were meant to be mine,
But I just walked away,
And I don't know why.

V2
You can't get so deep,
I won't let you,
You can't go so far,
I will stop you.

V3
My heart keeps poundin',
My body's swayin',
I see what's in your eyes,
But I just can't say goodbye.

CHORUS
Coz they're Crimes of Passion,
They're crimes of the heart,
Coz they're Crimes of Passion,
They'll tear you apart.

V4
You keep on chasin' me,
And I keep letting you go,

You're always askin' me why,
I say I don't know.

V5
I'm always runnin' away,
I just don't wanna get involved,
We're just like Adam and Eve,
When the earth first evolved.

REPEAT V3
My heart keeps poundin',
My body's swayin',
I see what's in your eyes,
But I just can't say goodbye.

ROCK MUSIC

V1
If you're not careful,
It can take control of your heart,
If you're not careful,
It can tear you apart.

V2
It really digs so deep,
And pulls you inside out,
It just makes your mind go crazy,
And you just gotta get out.

V3
You just can't stop yourself,
It really gets you goin',
You just can't stop yourself,
You gotta keep on movin'.

CHORUS
Coz it's so loud…
It's so good…
It's what ya call…
Rock Music…
So loud…
So good…
What ya call…
Rock Music…

V4
The excitement in the air,
Makes your pulse run,
The music everywhere,
Makes your heart pump.

REPEAT V2
It really digs so deep,
And pulls you inside out,
It just makes your mind go crazy,
And you just gotta get out.

REPEAT V3
You just can't stop yourself,
It really gets you goin',
You just can't stop yourself,
You gotta keep on movin'.

MOVIN' ALONG
ballad

This song was inspired by Debbie Gibson's *Foolish Beat,* her first #1 single from the Out Of The Blue album.

V1
The day we broke up,
My heart split in two,
You said you didn't love me,
I guess I knew we were through.

V2
I keep aching inside,
Every time I think of you,
Though I know we're finished…
I'll never stop dreaming of you.

V3
I keep on hurting inside,
Though you don't love me anymore,
It's really tearing me apart,
But there's only one thing I can do.

CHORUS
I'm not wanted anymore,
I was just like a toy,
When you were finished with me,
You just threw me away, oh boy,

Since no one wants me no more,
I guess I'll just keep Movin' Along…

V4
I guess it's got to happen,
I've gotta get you out of my mind,
And though times are changing,
I guess love isn't easy to find…

REPEAT V2
I keep aching inside,
Every time I think of you,
Though I know we're finished…
I'll never stop dreaming of you.

THE HEAVENS ARE BURNING

This song was inspired by the goings on in the world at the time. Back in 1989 the climate was all about CFCs and the hole in the ozone layer. And if you look closely at the lyrics in versus 3 and 4, we're still talking about some of the same issues today.

V1
What's happening to the world today?
What are we all saying?
If we don't do somethin' soon,
What will we all be doing?

V2
The world's burning up slowly,
Decomposing just like trash,
Life on earth will go by quickly,
And soon it will all be a flash.

CHORUS
The Heavens Are Burning,
Burning so quickly,
Whatever we're going to do,
We have to do it soon,
Because the heavens are burning,
Burning all lifeforms,
Life on earth will be one big storm.

V3
The seas are rising slowly,
The ice is always melting,
If we don't do somethin' soon,
We'll all be drowning.

V4
The hole is getting bigger,
Slowly day by day,
The pollution is getting thicker,
Smothering us in every way.

CHORUS

V5
The trees are being chopped down,
Don't you know they keep us alive?
If we all work together,
Maybe we can really survive.

V6
Life and earth is disintegrating,
We just can't tell a lie,
If we don't do somethin' soon,
We're just all gonna die.

DANGER ZONE

V1
I didn't know…
That love was so strong,
I never thought…
That it was all wrong.

V2
You shouldn't cross my heart,
It's not the thing to do,
You shouldn't think that way,
It's the wrong thing to do.

V3
Stay away from me,
You might get me mad,
You might break my heart,
And bad boys can't do that.

CHORUS
Don't cross that line,
It's a Danger Zone…
Don't cross my heart,
Coz it's a Danger Zone…
Don't cross my feelings,
Coz they're a Danger Zone…
Don't break my heart,
It's a Danger Zone…

V4
Don't come near me,
Guys make me mad,
Steer clear from me,
Boys like you shouldn't be bad.

CHORUS

BRIDGE
Don't cross my feelings,
Don't cross that line,
Don't break my heart,
Don't waste my time.

BEWARE

I have a feeling this song was inspired by Indecent Obsession's *Never Really Loved You.*

V1
The day you walked into my life,
I knew you were the one,
We're so right together,
But I just wanted some fun.

V2
I keep you hangin' on,
You never leave my side,
You kept on hangin' round,
Were you takin' me for a ride?

V3
So won't you give me all your love,
Maybe it's what I need…
Baby I love you so,
But you know I can't be freed…
From this love.

CHORUS
Beware! My heart is full of love so,
Beware! That love is all for you,
Beware! I don't know what I will do,
Beware!

V4
You tell me that you love me,
You tell me that you care,
You say you'll never leave me,
You say you'll always be there…

V5
You keep on hanging round,
I'm always getting away,
I think I love you boy,
I might get my way.

REPEAT V3
So won't you give me all your love,
Maybe it's what I need…
Baby I love you so,
But you know I can't be freed…
From this love.

WANTED

This song was inspired by Kylie Minogue's *Love At First Sight.* One of her better songs as they kinda went bad after her pop years.

V1
Everything was so perfect,
The day you looked at me,
I knew you were the one,
Oh, boy can't you see.

V2
Our lives were made this way,
As it was meant to be,
We were made for each other,
You're supposed to love me.

V3
There's things that you can do,
You've gotta love me too,
Oh, I want you boy,
I'm not being coy.

CHORUS
You're a Wanted man,
You're Wanted for love,
I want you for everything,
Won't you give me all your love?

V4
We were meant to be together,
Oh, boy don't you know,
Together means forever,
I just gotta let you know.

V5
I love you so much,
I won't let you go,
Won't you give me all your love?
I gotta tell you so.

REPEAT V3
There's things that you can do,
You've gotta love me too,
Oh, I want you boy,
I'm not being coy.

HERE TODAY, GONE TOMORROW

This song was inspired by Pseudo Echo's *Don't You Forget*. I had been a fan of PE's since 1985, and 1989 was a new sound as well as a new look for them. Longer hair, edgier music, ripped jeans. They were going for the American rock band look, so far from their pop days.

V1
What's been happening?
Years are going by so quickly,
We were young yesterday,
But we're aging so quickly.

V2
First the man on the moon,
And then the Beatles' tunes…
But that was all in the past,
These times are going so fast.

V3
Now we're in the computer age,
Will we still remember…?
When robots take over,
What happened in the past was meant forever.

CHORUS
Coz it's Here Today and Gone Tomorrow,
Times are changing so fast,
Here Today and Gone Tomorrow,
Are we going to forget our past?

V4
What's going to happen?
In these times to come?
What's going to happen?
Now the damage has been done?

V5
We're going into a new age,
Of robots and computers,
Coming out of the olden days,
Will we still remember?

YOU'RE ON YOUR WAY
ballad

I have a feeling this one was inspired by a Pseudo Echo song, *Searching For Glory*, but I can't be sure.

V1
You're workin' seven days a week,
Tryin' to make it through,
You're workin' day to day,
Tryin' to start anew.

V2
Workin' hard's tough,
But you gotta start from somewhere,
Even if it's at the bottom,
It's gonna get you everywhere.

V3
I know life's not easy…
And you gotta do more,
But if you don't work hard,
What do we really work for?

CHORUS
You're On Your Way to the top,
If you wanna start,
You gotta work your way up,
You're On Your Way to the top,

You gotta start from somewhere,
If you wanna get to the top.

V4
You've got to start at the bottom,
If you wanna get to the top,
You have to work hard,
If you wanna go up.

V5
That's the way life is,
You don't get things for free,
You've got to work for what you want,
So you gotta work hard you see.

ON TOP

V1
Everything's going so right,
You made it to the top,
It's that time in your life,
When your spirits are goin' up.

V2
You're On Top of the world,
You're really on a high,
You've got everything you want,
Just don't say goodbye.

V3
You feel good about yourself,
Forever going somewhere,
You feel good in yourself,
Forever on the run.

CHORUS
You're On Top of everything,
You're On Top of the world,
You're On Top of your lovin' feelings,
You're On Top of the world.

V4
I'm really happy for you,
Your life's just not the same,

You've made something for yourself,
Please let's stop this game.

V5
I don't want to see you go,
You're now at the top,
Please don't say goodbye,
You've made your way up.

REPEAT V3
You feel good about yourself,
Forever going somewhere,
You feel good in yourself,
Forever on the run.

PLAYING UP

V1
You had such a good life,
Why did it all stop?
You were goin' so well,
Why did you start playing up?

V2
What's the matter with you?
You started going down,
Where have you been?
I haven't seen you around.

V3
What's wrong with you?
What are you doing?
You shouldn't go through hell,
The drugs just keep on going.

CHORUS
Playing Up,
You know you shouldn't do it,
You shouldn't play up,
You can't keep on going,
Playing Up.

V4
You've changed so much,
You always get mad,
Your life's in turmoil,
You're getting so bad.

V5
Your life's going downhill,
Always on the run,
You've almost reached the bottom,
What have you done?

V6
There's no hope for you now,
Unless you help yourself,
Why don't you do something,
Before you kill yourself?

IT'S OUR HOME

Another song inspired by the world we lived in, in 1989. At the time, I could see this as Australia's very own version of Band Aid's *Do They Know It's Christmas*, or USA for Africa's *We Are The World*, with Aussie singers and musos. I thought big back then, and still do. And the only note I had on this song was that it was going on Album 1. I thought ahead of myself at the time. I had my albums all planned out with which songs were going on them. Even though I couldn't sing.

V1
What have we all done?
This isn't the place it used to be,
What's been happening?
What does this change mean?

V2
Things just aren't what they seem,
They've been changing for a while,
The world's so different now,
It's been changing for a long time.

V3
So why don't you, Stand up and fight,
Coz we've got the right, To save our world.

CHORUS
It's Our Home and we don't wanna lose it,
It's Our Home and it always has been,
It's Our Home and it always will be our home.

V4
If we don't stand up and have a say,
There'll be nothing left for us,
The world could be coming to an end,
What will be left for us?

REPEAT V3
So why don't you, Stand up and fight,
Coz we've got the right, To save our world.

CHORUS

BRIDGE
We've gotta save our world,
And save it soon,
Or our children will have nothing,
We've gotta save our world,
And save it quickly,
Before another decade passes by.

ECHO OF YOUR LOVE
ballad

This song was inspired by Kylie Minogue's *Je Ne Sais Pas Pourquoi.* Not in the French way, just lyrically. So many of her songs and film clips were simple and easy back then.

V1
Now that you've gone,
My life is not the same,
We were so close,
Now you've gone away.

V2
I miss you so much,
But you're still in my heart,
The fights we use to have,
Really tore us apart.

V3
I still love you,
Each and every day,
I still want to,
Love you in every way.

CHORUS
It's an Echo of Your Love,
Full of you in every way,

The Echo of Your Love,
Reminds me of you every day.

V4
What am I supposed to do,
Now I'm on my own,
How could you do it to me?
You've left me all alone.

V5
Now that you've gone,
There's nothing left to do,
I've been left on my own,
It's not the same without you.

REPEAT V3
I still love you,
Each and every day,
I still want to,
Love you in every way.

WHO'S SORRY NOW?

V1
You wanted more,
More than I could give,
You hurt me more,
More than you could love.

V2
You said it all,
All that you could say,
I wanted more,
Now you're running away.

V3
You caused all the heartache,
You caused all the pain,
You caused all the fighting…

CHORUS
Who's Sorry Now?
You left me for another,
Who's Sorry Now?
It's one or the other.

V4
I really guessed it,
Guessed it in every way,
You already knew it,

Knew it every day.

V5
How could you do it?
Do it to me that way,
Why did you leave me?
Why did you run away?

REPEAT V3
You caused all the heartache,
You caused all the pain,
You caused all the fighting…

LET'S PARTY

The only note I had written on this song was that it was going to be a B-side single to one of my many hits.

V1
Everybody gather round,
There's a party going on,
Bring all your friends around,
We're really gonna get down.

V2
Don't come alone,
Everyone's gonna be there,
Don't come on your own,
Lots of people will be there.

V3
Come on and really groove,
It's gonna be good tonight,
You can really get on down,
You can do it all tonight.

CHORUS
Let's Party tonight,
We're gonna have a good time,
Let's Party all night,
It's gonna be so right.

V4
Are you having a good time?
You know how to move,
The party's really going,
You can really groove.

REPEAT V2
Don't come alone,
Everyone's gonna be there,
Don't come on your own,
Lots of people will be there.

CHORUS

BRIDGE
Won't you tell me something,
Are you having fun?
Go on tell me one thing,
Is this really fun.

1990

I was 16 and out of school, listening to more, doing more, and reading more. So more artists were in my life and I was starting to analyse song lyrics. Which I guess led me to analyse books. Here are the 52 songs I wrote in 1990.

ONLY IN MY DREAMS

This song was inspired by Debbie Gibson's *Only In My Dreams*, hence the same name. Titles cannot be copyrighted so many people use the same titles for many things such as books and songs, which is why it can also get confusing when trying to find the right one. I'm also listening to it on my iPod right now as I type this.

V1
When I dream about you,
Good things happen to me,
When I dream about you,
It's like it was meant to be.

V2
Dreams are just like secrets,
I keep them to myself,
My dreams keep going round 'n round,
But I don't tell no one else.

CHORUS
Only In My Dreams,
I dream about you,
Only In My Dreams,
Do dreams come true?
As real as it may seem,
It's Only In My Dreams.

V3
And when I look into your eyes,
It's a fantasy come true,
Though you don't know how I feel,
I know I love you.

V4
When dreams come true,
It's a magical time,
But it never happens to me,
Why can't you be mine?

CHORUS

BRIDGE
When my dreams come true,
I will be with you,
We will be together,
Even if it's Only In My Dreams,
As lonely as it seems,
It's Only In My Dreams.

BUSY SIGNAL

I rewrote this song in 1990. No idea why, but there must have been a reason. I think Swatch Watch names were an inspiration…but then that's just me…finding inspo in anything.

V1
What's happening behind your lit windows?
Are there secrets you're hiding from me?
You haven't been acting yourself,
So please won't you show me…

V2
I've known now for a while,
Something's been going on,
You don't wanna see me no more,
Won't you tell me what went wrong?

CHORUS
And when I phone,
I know you're home,
But all I get is a Busy Signal,
You never call,
But that's not all,
Coz when I want you all I get is a,
Busy Signal.

V3
I can't wait much longer,
So won't you tell me true,
Is there any danger,
That I could lose you?

V4
Is there someone else?
Who has caught your eye?
Is it something else?
I know you wouldn't lie.

CHORUS

BRIDGE
Oh boy won't you tell me now,
Before you break my heart,
That there is no chance,
That we will ever part.

TRULY OUTRAGEOUS

This song was inspired by Debbie Gibson's *Electric Youth* and rewritten in 1990. I also have the feeling there could be some Jem and The Holograms and Swatch Watch inspo going on as well.

V1
In the beginning it was just a dream,
Never knowing what it might mean,
If you dance you cannot stop,
Vibrating moods they go to the top.

V2
There is always music everywhere,
Coz you can't fight it,
Why don't you live by it?
It's a world of passion,
A world of pain,
And if it gets to you,
You'll never be the same.

CHORUS
It's a wild world of rock 'n roll,
Right across the nation,
Sending people out of control,
In every civilisation,
Making you feel emotions,
Until you get the notion,

It's Truly Outrageous,
In a wild world of rock 'n roll.

V3
When you're in the spotlight,
It's where you want to be,
You know it's what you want,
Just you wait and see.

V4
It's a new sensation,
Being starry-eyed,
In the starlight,
And you know it feels oh so right.

CHORUS

BRIDGE
You know things aren't what they seem,
We're all looking for the world of reality,
Glamour and glitter, fashion and fame,
It never comes naturally,
It's never the same…
Would you give up your security?
For just the possibility,
That you could be a part,
Of this wild world of rock n roll.

COMPETING TO WIN

This one was inspired by John Farnham's *Playing To Win*, and Debbie Gibson's *Should've Been The One*. A very weird combination, musically.

V1
The last time I saw you,
You were in her arms real tight,
The last thing I heard about you,
You were with her all night.

V2
Oh baby I was unlucky last time,
But things are gonna change,
Oh baby you're gonna be mine,
I won't be late this time.

CHORUS
This time, I'm not gonna lose,
This time, I'll change my views,
This time, I'm not gonna lose your love…
Coz I'm Competing to Win,
Now I'm gonna get my way,
Competing To Win,
I won't wait another day,
Competing to Win,
I'm not gonna be late this time,
Oh baby let me change your mind…

V3
When it comes to the truth,
You took second best,
You didn't think things through,
You thought you knew what was best.

V4
Because I waited too long,
There was nothing I could say,
There was nothing I could do,
And in the end I had to pay.

CHORUS

BRIDGE
But now I've realised,
And I've changed my views,
I'm gonna do something,
I ain't got nothin' to lose.

WIN OR LOSE
rap

This song was inspired by Indecent Obsession's rap song *Goin' Down,* from their first album, Spoken Words. So when you read it, rap it.

V1
Everybody thinks they know what's right,
But when you think about it,
You're gonna have to see the light,
People tell you this,
People tell you that,
What are you meant to do?
You gotta follow all the facts.

CHORUS
You're gonna Win Or Lose,
That's how you play the game,
You don't do what others do,
You don't have to do the same,
Win Or Lose,
You're gonna have to take a chance,
Win Or Lose,
It's what you call romance.

V2
They say they know about love,
They know about romance,

And when it comes down to it,
They say you have to take a chance,
You gotta play by the book,
That's what you have to do,
And if you wanna get things right,
Here's what you're gonna do.

CHORUS

BRIDGE
Woh, oh, oh,
You're gonna Win Or Lose,
You have to take a chance,
You're gonna Win Or Lose,
When you find some real romance.

CHORUS

V3
You gotta do what you feel,
And you have to do it right,
If you want the one you love,
You gotta get up and fight,
People tell you this,
People tell you that,
Don't worry about them,
Don't follow all the facts.

FOREVER IN TIME
ballad

This song was inspired by Debbie Gibson's *No More Rhyme.* I wrote simple short sentences, but they made for long verses, that's just the way I wrote them. So I've doubled up the sentences to fit them in here.

V1
There's a place, in our lives,
Where we'll go, but not to hide,
There's a fact, we have to face,
We can't lie, to save ourselves,
We can talk, about each other,
But will there be…another time…

CHORUS1
When we are near,
And so close to one another,
It seems so unreal,
That we can have,
Such love in our lives…
And it will be, Forever in Time.

V2
When the fear sets in, When the love has gone,
When the memories fade, Will we still live on…?
We can ask ourselves, If we still remember,
The good times from the past,

When we were together,
But I still hope, in my mind,
That there will be…another time…

CHORUS2
Can we speak the truth?
About the times we had,
The things that we had done,
The love that we had shared,
Or am I still hoping…
That there will be…another time.

V3
We can't run, anymore,
From the truth, in our hearts…
The future's ahead, For both me and you,
We know what's best, What we can do…
We'll go our separate ways,
But we both know,
Our love's on the line…
But will there be…another time…

CHORUS3
Can we speak the truth?
About the times we had,
The things that we had done,
The love that we had shared,
Or am I still hoping…
That it will be…Forever in Time.

BEFORE DAY BREAKS

Another song that was going to be a B-side for one of my many hits.

V1
Tonight's gonna be the night,
Coz everything will be oh so right,
We're gonna have a good time,
And it's gonna be oh so fine.

V2
We'll invite everyone around,
Have some dancin' and get on down,
So come on over and don't be last,
Coz this night's gonna be such a blast.

CHORUS
We'll have the time of our lives,
Before Day Breaks,
We'll be up all night,
Before Day Breaks,
It'll be oh so right,
Before Day Breaks.

V3
It's gonna be the night of the year,
So don't worry never fear,
You and I will be together,

It'll be one time that we'll remember.

V4
Don't worry you will find,
It's really gonna blow your mind,
Everyone will be there,
So have some fun if you dare.

EYES OF FIRE

Inspired by Indecent Obsession's *Take Me Higher,* a B-side single to a hit.

V1
I fell in love,
The first time I saw you,
I don't know what it is,
That drew me to you.

V2
When I'm with you,
It all seems unreal,
But when I look into your eyes,
I know how I feel.

CHORUS
When I look at you,
All I see are those Eyes of Fire,
And when you look at me,
I can see that they're filled with desire,
Oh baby you take me higher,
When you look at me with those…
Eyes of Fire.

V3
You've drawn me like a magnet,
That's how you want it to be,

I can see it in your eyes,
When you look at me.

V4
There's a connection,
That's so strong,
When we're together,
It can't be wrong.

CHORUS

BRIDGE
There's something about you,
I guess it's the look in your eye,
Coz when you looked at me,
You caught my eye.

DESTINY

V1
It was Destiny,
That brought us together,
The day we met,
Don't you remember?

V2
We can't deny,
What was true,
The way we felt,
But we both knew.

CHORUS
It was always Destiny,
We were meant to be together,
It was always Destiny,
Together means forever,
It's just a part of history,
It was meant to be,
Coz it's what you call Destiny.

V3
When you looked at me,
I was captivated,
And when you held me near,
Bad memories faded.

V4
Oh boy you were the one,
We both know I'm right,
You stole my heart,
In the heat of the night.

CHORUS

BRIDGE
It was Destiny,
That brought us together,
It was meant to happen,
Will it be forever?

CRAZY HEART
ballad

V1
She tries to do her best,
But her best won't do,
She works really hard,
Trying to see it through.

V2
She's running out of luck,
But she just can't see,
If she wants some romance,
She's gotta find the key.

V3
She thinks it's tough,
Trying to find someone,
But she'll get there in the end,
She'll be the lucky one.

CHORUS
She's got nothin' but a Crazy Heart,
She's always taking a chance,
She's got nothin' but a Crazy Heart,
When it comes to romance.

V4
She's taking chances all the time,
Never knowing what she'll find,
She needs a little bit of TLC,
From a special guy you see.

CHORUS

BRIDGE
She says she's through with love,
She says she doesn't care,
But if the right guy comes along,
He'll answer all her prayers.

FLAME IN MY HEART

V1
I never thought it would happen,
I guess I wasn't sure,
But up till now,
I never thought about it before.

V2
You came into my life,
And set my world on fire,
You showed me things,
And filled my soul with desire.

V3
You wanted more than love,
I'd never felt like this before,
You said it would be fine,
But I was never sure.

CHORUS
You light a Flame in My Heart,
When we're together,
You light a Flame in My Heart,
Will it be forever?
You set my world on fire,
The first time I saw you,
You came into my life,
And I knew that you,

You light a Flame in My Heart.

V4
I felt all the emotions,
I thought I never had,
You've lit up my world,
With the love we have.

CHORUS

BRIDGE
I have never felt this way,
But I know now it's true,
You light a flame in my heart,
When I'm with you.

IN LOVE WITH YOU

Inspired by Debbie Gibson's *We Could Be Together.*

V1
I don't know why,
I do the things I do,
My friends all say,
That I'm In Love With You.

V2
People say I'm crazy,
And I know it's true,
But I can't help myself,
Coz I'm In Love With You.

CHORUS
My family say I'm crazy,
And I know it's true,
The only thing is,
That I'm In Love With You,
You're out of this world,
You're just so special,
Oh boy you know it's true,
I'm In Love With You.

V3
You make me laugh,
And you make me cry,

You've made me feel things,
And I don't know why.

V4
I dream about you,
All the time,
You're in my thoughts,
Coz I know you're mine.

CHORUS

BRIDGE
My time's taken up,
With the things we do,
I want you near me,
Coz I'm In Love With You.

FOLLOW YOUR DREAMS

Inspired by Debbie Gibson's *Over The Wall*, and Indecent Obsession's *Believe*, which is still my absolute favourite I.O. song. It's upbeat, catchy, and so poppy and danceable. I still listen to it today even though it was on their first album in 1989.

V1
You have to believe in yourself,
If you want your dreams to come true,
Don't worry about no one else,
Just do what you want to do.

V2
No matter how long you dream,
You can get to the top,
You got to put yourself first,
Then don't ever stop.

V3
People will pull you down,
Don't let them get to you,
You can get far ahead,
And have your dreams come true.

CHORUS
You've got to Follow Your Dreams,
If you believe in yourself,

Dreams can true,
But you've got to think of you,
You've got to Follow Your Dreams,
If you want to get somewhere,
No matter how big or small,
You can have it all.

V4
You've got to be happy in yourself,
And strive for what you need,
You can have what you want,
And you can be what you want to be.

CHORUS

BRIDGE
You want your life to be good,
So follow what's in your heart,
Your dreams can come true,
But you've got to make a start.

LOVIN' FOOL

V1
You wanted some love in your life,
But you never had to try,
It never seemed to end,
And you were wondering why.

V2
You were always taken for a ride,
Never knowing what to do,
You went from one love to another,
Never knowing what was true.

V3
You were always playing games,
Never being true to your heart,
You were trying to be so cool,
And inside you were being torn apart.

CHORUS
Coz you're a Lovin' Fool,
Trying to act so cool,
Lovin' Fool,
You think you know it all,
Coz you're a Lovin' Fool,
Always playing games,
Lovin' Fool,
Never knowing what you'll gain.

V4
You've had so many loves,
You've told so many lies,
You've gone to so many places,
On hot summer nights.

CHORUS

BRIDGE
There's real love to be found,
But you've got to find what's right,
There's someone out there,
For you day or night.

LOVE IN YOUR EYES

Inspired by Debbie Gibson's *Lost In Your Eyes,* hence the similar name. As with *Only In My Dreams*, titles can be used by anyone and are not copyrighted.

V1
I knew it was love,
When I first looked at you,
You were the one,
I knew it was true.

V2
I fell for you,
I knew it all along,
The look in your eyes,
Made me feel like I belonged.

CHORUS
You know there's Love in Your Eyes,
Oh boy I can see that there's,
Love in Your Eyes,
When you look at me,
Was it meant to be?
Because I'm mad about you.

V3
Oh I know in my heart,
That something's there,

Is it the love I'm in?
Or because you really care.

V4
I know that what I feel,
Is reflected in your eyes,
You showed me what was real,
And took me to the skies.

CHORUS

BRIDGE
I was lost in heaven,
With love and passion,
But then I knew,
That this love is for me and you.

AS TIME GOES BY

After re-reading these lyrics I'm thinking there's some Swatch Watch inspo going on.

V1
I'll set my sights higher,
Higher than the stars,
I want to live a story truer than the truth,
But it's been hard.

V2
We both have beating hearts,
Dreaming of secret lives,
We know how we love to live,
And we've been taken to the skies.

CHORUS
As Time Goes By,
Don't betray any emotions,
It's the perfect disguise,
Repeating a forgotten music,
As Time Goes By,
We won't forget the notion,
Innocence can be so tempting,
But so are the spirits that rise.

V3
I'm searching for a magic gate,
That will lead my way to you,
And will open up to the future,
And show me what is true.

V4
Day after day at every minute,
Hand in hand before day breaks,
We'll talk and talk for hours,
And make up for all our mistakes.

CHORUS

BRIDGE
The only thing that is the same,
Is a spirit hiding behind itself,
As seasons change so do the colours of nature,
But only in a book behind the shelf.

SHELTER IN THE STORM
ballad

V1
The world's so big,
I can't help feeling lost,
People fighting for themselves,
Never thinking of the cost.

V2
But I know I'll get by,
If you're by my side,
And I know in your arms,
I'll find some place to hide.

CHORUS
You are the one,
Who makes my world so safe and bright,
You are my beacon, you are my light,
You are the one,
When you are near in every way,
I'm not afraid to face each day,
Yes you are the one,
You are my Shelter In The Storm.

V3
I act so brave,
But at times I feel so small,
And when I'm alone,

That's when I need you most of all.

V4
With your love,
I know I'm gonna be all right,
All I need is your love,
Every day and every night.

DON'T SHED A TEAR

There's more Swatch Watch name inspo going on here and there's some Debbie Gibson somewhere I think.

V1
It's time again,
To look into your eyes,
But all I see is the same thing,
Golden lightning in a stormy sky.

V2
It hasn't been the same,
Since we broke apart,
It's like being in a dream,
But who's gonna make a start.

CHORUS
So don't…
So Don't Shed A Tear…
Coz it ain't worth crying for,
That's what love is all about,
It ain't worth crying for,
So don't ever have a doubt…

V3
I thought we had so much time,
There was always music in the air,
Don't you remember when,

You were always gonna be there…

V4
We've got to take a step ahead,
Because we can't go back,
To the time when our love was new,
But that is all in the past.

CHORUS

BRIDGE
You know one thing,
Money isn't everything that's for sure,
And even though we had each other,
We always looked for more.

WISH UPON A STAR
ballad

Here's another B-side single. I clearly knew what was good and what was B-side grade when I wrote my songs.

V1
I looked in the mirror,
And what did I see,
I saw all the love,
Reflecting in me.

V2
What would I do,
If a genie appeared,
To make all my wishes come true...
If I had three wishes,
I wouldn't need two,
But who needs wishes to spare?

CHORUS
All I'd have to do is,
Wish Upon A Star,
Just to see how far I'd go,
Wish Upon A Star,
I wouldn't have to go far,
For your love.

V3
Listen to your heart,
And take some good advice,
Then I won't have to ask you,
And I won't have to tell you twice.

V4
All I had to do,
Was just look at you,
To feel what was true,
And that's when I first knew.

CHORUS

REPEAT V2
What would I do,
If a genie appeared,
To make all my wishes come true…
If I had three wishes,
I wouldn't need two,
But who needs wishes to spare?

LET'S ROCK THIS TOWN

Definitely inspired by Debbie Gibson's *Electric Youth* and a Jem and The Holograms outfit. Yep, a song inspired by an outfit name…

V1
People runnin' round 'n round,
Not knowing where to go,
Feel your body gettin' down,
You really can't let go, oh no,
We may be young but we all know,
We can do anythin' so come on let's go.

CHORUS 1
Let's Rock This Town,
And make the world go round,
Let's Rock This Town,
We'll make you listen to our sound,
Come on, get down,
Masterminded by the young,
We'll rock this town.

V2
We have our thoughts and we have our rights,
Don't ever forget that we know what's right,
We don't know everything that's for sure,
But give us a chance and we could learn more.

CHORUS 2
Let's Rock This Town,
And make the world go round,
Let's Rock This Town,
We'll make you listen to our sound,
Come on get down,
We're the next generation,
We'll rock this town.

BRIDGE
We'll drive you crazy with all our words,
We'll make you listen to us,
Coz we wanna be heard,
Oh yeah…
We're full of energy and we're comin' on strong,
So come on let us try coz we know we belong…
To the future…

ONCE IN A LIFETIME

This could have been inspired by Debbie Gibson's *Out Of The Blue*, but I just can't remember…

V1
When you walked into my life,
You were a perfect stranger,
But I didn't have to wait long,
To feel no danger.

V2
I had to love again,
But was it an emotional tie,
Having you was just so hard,
But I found a way to try.

CHORUS
It was Once In A Lifetime,
A new love that had come along,
I had taken chances…on romances,
But I knew that this wasn't wrong.

V3
You came into my life,
Out of the blue,
You showed me love,
And changed my point of view.

V4
I was under the spell,
You had captured me in,
You took my breath away,
Time and time again.

CHORUS

BRIDGE
With all your love,
You set my heart on fire,
And made my soul,
Fly higher and higher.

NOW AND FOREVER
ballad

Inspired by Debbie Gibson's Silence Speaks A Thousand Words.

V1
Remember that night,
That night in September,
The rain was pouring down,
As if it would never…stop.

V2
There were golden moments,
I'll never forget,
The night our love became one,
And I thought it would always go on.

CHORUS
Now and Forever,
Our love was so new,
And I thought it would be,
Now and Forever,
You said it was true,
That it always would be,
Now and Forever.

V3
You said you had to leave,
I never wanted to be on my own,
You said it could be over,
I didn't want to live a lifetime alone.

V4
Maybe it was a season of passion,
I shouldn't have expected it to last,
As our time together came to an end,
What we had slipped into the past.

CHORUS

BRIDGE
I'll never forget what we shared,
Even though I thought it would last forever,
But I'll always remember that night,
That night in September,
When the rain was pouring down,
And I thought we would always be together.

LOVIN' YOU

Inspired by Debbie Gibson's *Helplessly In Love* and *Love In Disguise* from the album Electric Youth.

V1
Why do we keep pretending,
Our love is never-ending,
But is there a way to survive?
I thought I knew you,
Like I knew myself,
You had showed me love like no one else.

V2
I always thought we'd be together,
I always thought together meant forever,
So won't you come and escape,
We'll make no mistake,
I always thought it was fate when we met.

CHORUS
I thought our love was so real,
Maybe it's just the way I feel,
But you know I always will,
Keep on Lovin' You,
We're like stars in the sky,
Baby we'll get by,
But you know I'll always try,
To keep on Lovin' You.

V3
Was your love just a disguise?
I thought I saw it in your eyes,
You know I speak the truth,
I'll give you proof but,
We can work it out,
You know I have no doubt.

V4
You know I cannot wait,
There are chances to take,
I need you in my arms,
Oh I knew it from the start,
Even when we were apart,
I knew you had stolen my heart.

CHORUS

BRIDGE
We're running out of time,
So let me throw you a line,
Take me back into your life,
Like I know you will,
Coz you know it's just as real as I do…oooohhh.

JUST TOO LATE
ballad

Inspired by Debbie Gibson's *Shades Of The Past*. Quite an unusual title for the time.

V1
You had promised me...
That it would be forever...
You had whispered to me...
That you would remember...
The times we had,
The love we'd shared,
But now I have to leave that all behind me...

CHORUS
You looked into my eyes and promised forever,
Was it just a disguise?
It's too hard to remember,
I have to make a choice, right now,
But I realise, it's Just Too Late...

V2
If I had only known...
What was in my heart...
If you had only known...
The truth from the start...
You're asking a lot,
Now we have to stop,

Because you want to be free…

CHORUS

V3
You had brought me red roses,
They were not enough,
You had wrote me love songs,
Though they were never of love…
I needed something stronger,
I couldn't wait much longer,
So I said goodbye to our love…

SEARCHING

Inspired by Debbie Gibson's *Fallen Angel*, my favourite song from the Out Of The Blue album.

CHORUS
I'm Searching in the dark,
I'm Searching for your heart,
But I know it's so hard to find,
Just a little peace of mind,
When I'm Searching for your love.

V1
I don't wanna be left alone,
So won't you stay with me?
Please don't leave me on my own,
So please don't go.

V2
I need all your love,
But you think it's enough,
I need you by my side,
For the rest of my life.

CHORUS

V3
You tell me it's time to go,
I don't wanna face the truth,

I might just lose you,
But not if I give you proof.

V4
Our love is true,
That's something we can't deny,
But now I've been Searching,
And I don't know why.

CHORUS

BRIDGE
You're trying to throw our love away,
But I'm not gonna let it go,
I'll keep Searching till the end of time,
Until your love will show.

BURNING UP

Inspired by Debbie Gibson's *Red Hot* and **NOT** the Madonna song of the same name.

V1
I saw the love in your eye,
And then I saw you smile,
Your love's becoming too hot to handle,
But was it worth my while.

V2
There's a burning fire in my soul,
But you want more, a higher goal.

CHORUS
I'm Burning Up for your love,
I'm Burning Up for your arms around me,
Hotter than a fire, red hot desire,
I'm burning, yearning,
I'm Burning Up.

V3
Your love was so new (I'm burnin'),
There was nowhere to turn (I'm yearnin'),
Your love was so true (Hotter than a fire),
It made my fires burn (Red hot desire).

CHORUS

BRIDGE
Don't try to catch me I might fall,
But don't let me go if you want more,
You want me for your own, but I wanna be free,
You're tryin' to hold on but can't you see…

TELL ME NOW

Inspired by Debbie Gibson's *Between The Lines.*

V1
I never thought,
That it could happen,
I never realised,
That it was so.

V2
I never dreamed,
That dreams could come true,
It always seemed,
My dreams were of you.

V3
I've got to know how you feel,
I've got to know if this is real.

CHORUS
Tell Me Now if this love is true,
If it's all new,
Tell Me Now,
I soon realised the look in your eyes,
You're always on my mind.

V4
I saw that smile,
That special look,
That drove me,
Drove me wild.

V5
All my feelings,
All the emotions,
That we've hidden away,
Are now here to stay.

REPEAT V3
I've got to know how you feel,
I've got to know if this is real.

GET IT TOGETHER

Inspired by Debbie Gibson's *Staying Together*...you can't go boy!

V1
You said you wanted to be free,
But you didn't wanna go,
I said, 'boy what's it gonna be?'
You said you didn't know.

V2
I'm not gonna let you go,
Not this time,
I'm waiting for your love to show,
Then you're gonna be mine.

CHORUS
Get It Together,
Oh boy don't you know,
You've got to,
Get It Together,
Before I go,
Or love will leave you,
So Get It Together.

V3
I'm gonna stand up and fight,
For your love,

But I know you just might,
Say it's enough.

V4
But it's not over,
Coz there's something you should know,
You can wish all you want on a four leaf clover,
But I'm not gonna go.

CHORUS

REPEAT V2
I'm not gonna let you go,
Not this time,
I'm waiting for your love to show,
Then you're gonna be mine.

TREAT ME RIGHT

Inspired by Debbie Gibson's *Wake Up To Love* and Indecent Obsession's *Tell Me Something*.

INTRO
Hey boy,

V1
Let me tell you something,
You're not the boy you used to be,
We both know one thing,
You don't seem the same to me.

V2
I wanna know what happened,
Is it some sort of game?
Please tell me what changed,
It's never been the same…

CHORUS
Treat Me Right,
That's what you gotta do,
Treat Me Right,
You gotta love me too,
Treat Me Right,
Oh boy don't you know,
Treat Me Right,
And love won't go.

V3
You know you, were my best friend,
But then it seemed to end,
There was so much unnecessary pain,
But then it seemed love started again.

CHORUS

BRIDGE
Oh boy you know you're such a flirt…
But somebody just might get hurt,
Here's what you do, you gotta fight,
If you want me to stay, you gotta Treat Me Right.

TOGETHER AGAIN

Inspired by Debbie Gibson's *Out Of The Blue*.

V1
We've been apart,
For so long,
But now we're singing,
The same old song.

V2
It's happened,
Once before,
So many times,
But what's once more?

CHORUS
Now we're Together Again,
We were in love,
Now we're Together Again,
You know I can't forget,
But now we're Together Again.

V3
You were always there,
By my side,
But when we broke up,
You decided to hide.

V4
You couldn't admit,
What you felt,
But now we're together,
And in your eyes I'll melt.

CHORUS

BRIDGE
You tried to face your feelings,
And I needed to know,
About all your emotions,
And that you didn't wanna go.

GAMES OF LOVE

Inspired by Debbie Gibson's *Shake Your Love*.

V1
We've been playing games,
For some time now,
But what have we gained?
I just don't know now.

V2
Why didn't I see,
That I've been looking for clues,
It didn't occur to me,
But then I knew.

CHORUS
Games Of Love,
You know we're playing,
Games Of Love,
But now we're saying,
Games Of Love,
Aren't something new,
Games Of Love,
We're not being true.

V3
We weren't being true,
That's for sure,

We're still playing games,
Like we did before.

V4
We can't go on,
Like this anymore,
What's going on,
What's it all for.

CHORUS

BRIDGE
I had the key to your heart,
But while playing games,
We were being torn apart.

BROKEN DREAMS
ballad

Inspired by Debbie Gibson's *Foolish Beat*.

V1
You broke my heart,
When you went away,
I thought you had loved me,
For more than a day.

V2
I could see no light,
In your eyes,
But I looked at you,
And then I realised.

CHORUS
That they're just Broken Dreams,
It was so real at first…
Broken Dreams,
It meant so much to me,
But now they're just…
Broken Dreams.

V3
You turned away,
And I didn't know why,
You walked outta my life,

Because you never tried.

V4
I didn't need,
To disguise,
What was on my mind,
And in your eyes.

CHORUS

BRIDGE
There was something,
In the way you looked at me,
But you were sending signals,
Of insecurity.

COME BACK

Inspired by Indecent Obsession's ballad *Come Back To Me* from their 1989 album Spoken Words.

V1
Was it only a summer of love?
Because I thought we were more than friends,
Why couldn't it have been a lifetime of love?
But even though we tried it still seemed to end.

V2
Was it because I didn't love you baby?
Even though that's what you thought,
I really do, love you baby,
You are always in my thoughts.

CHORUS
Come Back baby, Come Back to me,
I'm gonna give you good lovin' this time,
Come Back baby, Come Back to me please…
I'm gonna make you mine.

V3
Were my expectations too high,
For your love and desire to reach,
Was I hoping way too high?
But I just wanted you to teach…me baby.

V4
I can't wait much longer,
So won't you please come back to me,
I haven't been able to see things clearly,
You know you mean so much to me.

CHORUS

BRIDGE
Step by step and inch by inch,
I'm gonna get you back, woh, oh,
Minute by minute and day after day,
I'm gonna get my way with you.

IMAGINE

V1
You can be a winner,
At any game you choose to play,
You can make money,
And always get your own way.

V2
It doesn't take much,
To use your own imagination,
It's not that hard,
You can have a new sensation.

CHORUS
Imagine,
You can be what you wanna be,
Imagine,
You can have what you please,
Imagine,
You can do what you wanna do,
Imagine,
You can have what you choose.

V3
You can be a pop star,
And be on tv,
You can be a movie star,
And have your face on the silver screen.

REPEAT V2
It doesn't take much,
To use your own imagination,
It's not that hard,
You can have a new sensation.

LIFE IN THE FASTLANE

Inspired by Debbie Gibson's *Who Loves Ya Baby*, Dannii Minogue's *Success* and Madonna's *Vogue*. Quite a musical mix.

V1
Success…
Isn't all what it seems,
Baby make sure,
You're not in a dream,
It can go, to your head,
If you let it,
You can get caught up in the clouds,
If you forget it.

V2
If you don't have enough time,
To look in the mirror,
Make sure you take note,
Of who loves you…

CHORUS
You've got a busy life,
Life In The Fastlane,
Not enough time to look around…
You've got a busy life,
Life In The Fastlane,
Keep yourself on the ground…

V3
You're not alone in this world of glamour,
You've got people who care for you,
Just remember who you are,
And who's always there for you.

REPEAT V2
If you don't have enough time,
To look in the mirror,
Make sure you take note,
Of who loves you…

CHORUS

BRIDGE
Limousines and beauty queens,
Magazines and silver screens,
Stages, ragers and players too,
You can have it all if you can get through…
The late nights and neon lights,
You can go places where black meets white…
It's doesn't matter who you are,
If your life is in the fastlane you can go far.

COUNTIN' THE DAYS

Inspired by Debbie Gibson's *Who Love's Ya Baby*, from the album Electric Youth.

V1
I'm all alone as I'm waiting for you,
You know I think about you every day,
Remembering what we have,
And how you showed me love in every way.

V2
You know I feel helpless,
Because I'm missin' you,
I can't see clearly,
Coz I miss kissin' you.

CHORUS
I'm Countin' The Days,
Till I see you again,
Wanting you here with me,
I'm Countin' The Days,
Till you're by my side,
I'm not gonna let you free.

V3
You've been gone so long,
I thought you would fade away,
But I know you'll come back,

When? It should be any day.

V4
I'm waiting to hold you in my arms,
But it's like you've been taken away,
I know that it's not for long,
But it's like forever and a day.

TEMPTATIONS

Inspired by Dannii Minogue's *Temptations* from the album Get Into You.

V1
It didn't take much,
To steal your heart away,
For you it was so easy,
It was just another day.

V2
You were so busy,
You didn't see what was wrong,
Or what was around you,
You had been blind for so long.

CHORUS
Temptations,
Have taken your heart away,
You stopped loving for one more day,
Temptations,
You had to have more,
But never really knowing what for.

V3
Your life was upside down,
But you didn't seem to care,
You had to have more,

Though I was always there.

V4
You turned away from me,
Because Temptations had taken your heart,
But I always loved you,
Even right from the start.

CHORUS

BRIDGE
Though it seems the magic has gone,
You had nothing left to say,
Even if a spark's still there,
I'll still be there every day.

A CRY IN THE NIGHT

This song was written for fur seals. Baby fur seals, which, in 1989, were beaten with a club to knock them out or kill them so their fur could be taken. Gross!

V1
You hear the sounds,
Loud against the night,
You hear the cries,
As they try to fight.

V2
They won't give up,
They're on a wing and a prayer,
Hoping someone will hear them,
Hoping someone will care.

CHORUS
It's A Cry in the Night, as they try to live,
A Cry in the Night, hoping something will give,
Hunted and slain, they're left in the rain,
They've gone away, never living for one more day.

V3
They'll look at the sky,
And wish on a star,
That they'll be left alone,
So they can go far.

V4
But the axe falls and another goes,
Just where to no one knows,
What will happen, will they survive?
To grow with life and stay alive.

CHORUS

BRIDGE
So they don't give up,
Knowing now, someone cares,
Their cries have been heard,
For someone is there.

YOU'D BETTER STOP

Inspired by Kylie Minogue's *Step Back In Time*, from the Rhythm Of Love album. Her early stuff was actually good, and very poppy for the era. I think Rhythm Of Love is my favourite album of hers.

V1
Take a step back in time,
And think about what's been done,
The laughter and tears that we shared,
When we were together as one.

V2
But times have changed,
And things just aren't the same,
It used to be so good,
But now there's just no flame.

CHORUS
You'd Better Stop if you love me,
We can't go on this way,
You'd Better Stop if you need me,
You know I won't go away,
You'd Better Stop, if you want me,
There's so much left to say,
You'd Better Stop, if you want to,
You know I'll be here every day.

V3
If you want me to stay,
You'd Better Stop and listen,
You say you love me,
When you see my eyes glisten.

V4
You say you want to stay,
But it seems we always fight,
I don't know what I will do,
When are you gonna see the light?

CHORUS

BRIDGE
I can't remember when,
You said we could start again,
But it all seems so long ago,
Well there's somethin' you should know.

DEVIL IN DISGUISE

Inspired by Kylie Minogue's *Better The Devil You Know*, which apparently was inspired by Michael Hutchence. It's also written about a certain member of Indecent Obsession.

V1
He'll take you in a moment,
With amazing speed,
He'll capture your heart,
Then you know you can't be freed.

V2
He has so much power,
But don't let him keep you down,
You try to get away,
Coz you know he'll be around.

CHORUS
He's the Devil in Disguise,
You see the look in his eyes,
He's the Devil in Disguise,
He'll make you realise,
He's the Devil in Disguise,
You know he'll electrify,
He's the Devil in Disguise,
Never ask him why.

V3
His love is so hot,
He'll set your soul on fire,
He'll fill you with passion,
And a burning desire.

V4
He'll make you take chances,
With a goal in mind,
He'll take you to the heavens,
But he knows you might find.

CHORUS

BRIDGE
He'll keep you hypnotised,
Coz he's a Devil in Disguise,
He'll make all your dreams come true,
But he's no angel, I guess you knew.

RED HOT LOVE

Inspired by Debbie Gibson's *Red Hot.*

V1
I feel your heart burning right through me,
But I don't believe it,
I feel your love just yearning for me,
And I know you can see it.

V2
I thought I was just dreaming,
But then I saw your eyes gleaming,
With passion and fire,
Oh you've taken me higher.

CHORUS
You've got Red Hot Love,
I can feel it,
Burning right through me,
You've got Red Hot Love,
Don't you know it,
You can see it too.

V3
I'm wondering if I can survive,
With your arms around me,
Oh when I look into your eyes,
Your vibes move through me.

V4
Baby I'm burning out of control,
I feel you have a hold on my soul,
Your heart fulfils my desire,
Just like a flame needs a fire.

CHORUS

BRIDGE
I thought I was just dreaming,
But then I saw your eyes gleaming,
Your heart fulfils my desire,
Just like a flame needs a fire.

SOMETHING TO DREAM
ballad

I have a feeling Debbie Gibson's *Only In My Dreams* inspired this one.

V1
I remember how things used to be,
And I realise that I miss you,
Things have changed so much,
If only I could kiss you.

V2
When things were over,
I thought we could start again,
I can't remember when I felt good,
No I can't remember when.

CHORUS
I need something to hope for,
I need Something to Dream,
I need a reason to have more,
How hard can it be?
I need Something to Dream.

V3
Our love was something real,
But I can't offer you proof,
Of why we should get back together,

And that is the total truth.

CHORUS

BRIDGE
Can't you see how much you mean to me?
Can't you see how much I care?
But now we're both free,
And you still mean the world to me,
I just want you to be there.

LOVE IS AN EMOTION

V1
It plays games with your heart,
And re-plays crazy dreams,
It's nothing no one says,
But we know it's as real as it seems.

V2
The emotions that we feel,
Are part of us emotionally,
And can cause such pain,
That can go on endlessly.

CHORUS
Love Is An Emotion,
I'll say it till you get the notion,
Love is the emotion,
That you can't push away,
Because it's here to stay,
For Love Is An Emotion.

V3
Can love be any clearer?
But it seems so complicated,
They say love isn't easy,
It seems so overrated.

V4
You may not always feel love,
But you know it's there subconsciously,
Your emotions wreak havoc,
You know that constantly.

CHORUS

BRIDGE
They can turn you inside out,
And take control of your heart,
They can put your mind in a whirl,
And then tear you apart.

WALLS OF FIRE

Inspired by Whitney Houston's *I'm Your Baby Tonight*.

V1
Oh when you touch me,
I'm in ecstasy,
And when you hold me near,
I lose all reality.

V2
Oh baby the look, in your eyes,
Makes me feel like,
I can do anything, anything
When you take me by surprise.

CHORUS
You've got Walls of Fire around you,
So much desire,
I've tried to break through,
You've got Walls of Fire around you,
You've taken me higher,
Coz it's a love that's true.

V3
You can call me crazy,
Or what you will,
But it will never change the way

That I will always feel.
V4
Oh baby when you look, at me with those eyes,
I just know,
I can do everything, everything,
That I've realised.

CHORUS

BRIDGE
I am taken, by your strength,
I've thought about it, at great length,
Oh you know you tie me, into a chain,
That's just something, I can't explain.

OPPOSITE EXTREMES

Inspired by Debbie Gibson's *Play The Field*, from Out Of The Blue.

V1
You were always dreaming,
About how you wanted things to be,
Your life had little meaning,
Why couldn't you open your eyes and see.

V2
That there is so much out there,
You got to find it somewhere,
There is so much you can do,
But you've got to follow it through.

CHORUS
You've taken things to the Opposite Extremes,
You were wasting your life on a dream,
Then you took things to the Opposite Extremes,
As unreal as it seems.

V3
You had burning desires,
You put them all behind,
You wanted to fly higher,
You know that you could find.

V4
You gotta look around,
Don't let it get you down,
There is so much waiting,
You just gotta start playing.

CHORUS

BRIDGE
You've got to set your mind,
Then things just might be fine,
Oh you can touch the sky,
Then you'll see that you can fly.

AN ANGEL'S DREAMS
ballad

Inspired by Dannii Minogue's *Don't Wanna Take This Pain* from the album Love and Kisses.

V1
I use to have such fantasies,
Of us being together,
I used to spend time all alone,
Wondering if it would be forever.

V2
I want you more than anything,
But what do I have to do?
I'm doing fine, but I have to take time,
To get my message through to you.

CHORUS
An Angel's Dreams,
Are higher than the heavens,
It's hard to believe,
In my wildest dreams, the passion.

V3
I've often wondered why,
It always took so long,
To turn your heart around,
But things went from right to wrong.

V4
I thought you were going to give,
But then you started again,
You were breaking my heart, so you'd better start,
If you wanna come back in.

CHORUS

BRIDGE
I'm gonna give you all my love,
No matter what you say,
I don't wanna take no more pain,
So please don't go away.

WITHOUT YOU
ballad

Inspired by Debbie Gibson's *Foolish Beat*.

V1
It started the day,
When I left you,
The pain and hurt,
It was all so new.

V2
The way you loved me,
It was all so good,
You loved me,
Like no one else could.

CHORUS
Now I'm Without You,
My life seems so empty,
I always thought that everything was fine,
Now I'm left Without You,
The pain goes on endlessly,
Our moments together have gone so fast,
There was a time when you were mine.

V3
Now it's a new time,
Now is a new place,

I can't forget you,
I always see your face.

V4
But now I'm so sorry,
And I realise I was wrong,
You slipped away,
Now you're gone.

CHORUS

BRIDGE
There was just no reasons,
For my actions,
It was too late to turn around,
I could never love again,
Coz I know it's at an end,
It's just gettin' me down.

FORGOTTEN DREAMS
ballad

V1
All I ever did was listen to your lies,
And when I saw no truth in your eyes,
I realised it was over.

V2
Yet I know I must be strong,
But how could I be so wrong,
I thought we'd always be together.

CHORUS
No matter what I do,
No matter what I say,
I seem to push you further away,
I feel so lost, but all I know,
Is that I've got to let go.

V3
I used to dream about me and you,
And I always thought we'd be true,
But now I'm so sorry.

V4
We used to have such good times,
How could I have been so blind?
But now I'm the one to worry.

CHORUS

BRIDGE
I always thought we were the best,
Even though we tried to pass the test,
I often wondered if you really cared,
You always said you were gonna be there,
Did I ever hear your shouts and screams,
Or were they in my mind, I guess not,
For now they're just Forgotten Dreams,
Oh please be good to me.

MESSENGER OF HOPE
ballad

Inspired by Debbie Gibson's *Deep Down* and *Miracle,* and Indecent Obsession's *Never Gonna Stop*.

V1
You turned your back on me,
And threw our love away,
But what did I do to you,
To make you turn so far away.

V2
You seemed to push yourself away from me,
Was it because of your friends?
You listened to them and not your heart,
Well our happiness all depends on you.

V3
Some people think love is impossible,
But sometimes it just needs a little miracle.

CHORUS
We need a Messenger of Hope,
I just don't know how I'm going to cope,
Without you here oh I need you near,
Where's our Messenger of Hope?
I've got to get on with my life,
I'm on a never-ending slide, oh I just can't hide.

V4
I was so sure, that I thought,
Everything was going to change,
I just cried and denied,
That my life had been rearranged.

V5
We need a little honesty but,
Your voice seems so crystal clear,
Then I see the look in your eyes,
I feel all my fears…returning.

V6
I think a little push and shove, give and take,
Is what we need coz I won't break.

CHORUS

BRIDGE
I always tried to be one step ahead,
But you know why you cut me down instead,
Deep down I know something was there,
Because it's something that felt so rare,
No matter how much harder I try,
I keep on asking myself why,
Something I thought was an impossibility,
Has turned into nothing but a mistaken tragedy.

RACE AGAINST TIME

Inspired by Indecent Obsession's *Say Goodbye,* and the world at the time, the children of the world, what we were doing with it, and what we could do to save it.

V1
All the children grow older,
More and more each day,
Just like the world we live in,
Growing older in every way.

V2
But they are our problems,
All our hopes and fears,
Which all get bigger,
As our world slowly disappears.

CHORUS
It's a Race Against Time,
Hoping our pleas will be heard,
As we try to save our world,
It's a Race Against Time,
We need more than just words,
This is our home, this is our world.

V3
What are we meant to do?
Listen to what people have to say,

Everyone treats it like a joke,
But this is no game that we play.

V4
We've got to do something now,
Before we run out of time,
We've got to get some action,
Or things won't be fine.

CHORUS

BRIDGE
There's nothing to score but a lifetime ahead,
We need something to be done,
More than what's been said.

EVERY TIME WE SAY GOODBYE

V1
Every Time We Say Goodbye,
It hurts more and more,
And Every Time We Say Goodbye,
It gets harder than before.

V2
But I know it won't be long,
Till I see you again,
I'll just have to wait,
I'll wait till then.

CHORUS
Now you're going away, and I just have to say,
That I want you to stay, if just for one more day,
You know my love is true, but we both knew,
It was just me and you, now I don't know what to do.

V3
Every Time We Say Goodbye,
It hurts to let you go,
And Every Time We Say Goodbye,
I gotta let you know.

V4
It won't be soon enough,
Till you're back with me,

I'll just have to wait,
I'll wait and see.

CHORUS

BRIDGE
It's so hard to say goodbye,
To the one you love,
But we'll get by, coz our love is strong,
It's enough.

I NEED SOMEONE

Inspired by Dannii Minogue's *True Lovers* and *Love And Kisses.*

CHORUS
I Need Someone,
I Need Someone,
I Need Someone to hold me tight,
I Need Someone,
I Need Someone,
I Need Someone to love me right.

V1
Hey boy, let's turn out the lights,
And love each other right,
It's magic when we're together,
Let's love all over again,
Coz you're more than just a friend,
I want it to be forever.

V2
I don't want a love that won't be,
Coz that's not the one for me.

CHORUS

V3
I don't wanna take chances,
On any other romances,
I don't want another,
You don't wanna break my heart,
I knew that from the start,
There is no other.

REPEAT V2
I don't want a love that won't be,
Coz that's not the one for me.

CHORUS

BRIDGE
People say that love is blind,
But I know I can spare the time,
We always said how we feel,
This is something I know is real.

CHORUS

REPEAT V2
I don't want a love that won't be,
Coz that's not the one for me.

ABOUT THE AUTHOR

Tiara burst into the world of publishing in 2011 and has blazed a trail ever since. Writing adult fiction as *L.J. Diva,* non-fiction and teen stories as *Tiara King,* and young adult stories as *T.K. Wrathbone,* she set up her own publishing house, *Royal Star Publishing,* to accommodate all of her books and multiple personalities.

Tiara's been creating jewellery and accessories since 1990, turned her obsessive love for it into her label, *Jewel Divas,* and writes at her style site, *Jewel Divas Style,* a one-stop blog for sparkling jewels, style, fun, and dancing under disco balls.

Tiara lives in Australia, has an obsession with colourful kaftans and kimonos, is a jewellery and sparkle addict, '80s music lover, and book collector.

SOCIALS

You can find more about Tiara on her website; follow her on social media, or visit her lifestyle blog, Jewel Divas Style, or her publishing house, Royal Star Publishing.

tiaraking.com.au

jeweldivasstyle.com

royalstarpublishing.com.au

Sign up for Tiara's Newsletter…

Make sure you're always in the know and never miss free exclusives, the latest news, book updates, and so much more with newsletters from…

tiaraking.com.au

HAVE YOU READ THESE?

SERIES

Poems Of A Musical Flavour: Volumes 1 – 6

MG/YA

#Teenblogger: To Follow or Not To Follow?

NON-FICTION

How To Be A Jewel Diva

Closet Confidential

Dream It, Write It, Publish It!

Unfulfilled

Tiara also writes sexy, sassy, kick-ass romances as L.J. Diva

tiaraking.com.au/ljdiva

And paranormal with a light twist of supernatural horror young adult as T.K. Wrathbone

tiaraking.com.au/tkwrathbone

www.ingramcontent.com/pod-product-compliance
Lightning Source LLC
Chambersburg PA
CBHW021108080526
44587CB00010B/436